Profitable New Quilting Business

Profitable New Quilting Business

Lee Lister is a Business Consultant with more than 25 year's consultancy experience for many household names. She is known as The Bid Manager or The Biz Guru.

From an early age she began an unparalleled journey through business consulting that continues to span across the UK, USA, Europe and Asia. She has consulted for many companies all over the world. Specialising in business change management, start up consultancy and trouble shooting. She is highly skilled in seminars, lectures and corporate presentations on business, project management and bid management. Lee's experience in marketing and internet marketing is also keenly sought after.

She is a prolific published writer of books, ebooks and articles on business, entrepreneurship and bid management. She can easily be found on major search engines and Amazon.

Profitable New Quilting Business

Profitable New Quilting Business

Learn how to set up a profitable business, understand how to overcome the strains and stresses of a new company and become a Successful Entrepreneur.

www.ProfitableNewBusiness.com

Author: Lee Lister

No part of this publication may be reproduced, stored in a retrieval system, or transmitted in any form or by any means, without the prior permission in writing of the publisher, nor be otherwise circulated in any form of binding or cover other than that in which it is published and without a similar condition including this condition being imposed on the subsequent purchaser. This book may not be used as a training course in any format.

Profitable New Quilting Business

Other books available include:

Entrepreneur's Apprentice

How Much Does It Cost To Start A Business?

Proposal Writing For The Smaller Businesses

Start My New Party Selling Business

Start My New Cake Decorating Business

Start My New Manicurist Business

Profitable New Face Painting Business

First published in Great Britain in 2009.

© Copyright Lee Lister 2009

All rights reserved.

Published by: Biz Guru Ltd

Photo Copyright: © Scott Williams

ISBN: 978-0-9563861-1-3

This book is dedicated to my daughter Kerry Lister for whom I have always strived to be my best.

Profitable New Quilting Business

Contents

Legal Notice -- 8

Introduction --------------------------------------- 10

Getting Your Business Started ----------------- 13

The Nasties -- 15

Will I Succeed? ----------------------------------- 16

A Successful Business Start up --------------- 19

Your Business Framework--------------------- 21

How Much Does It Cost To Start A Business? 24

Common Business Mistakes. ------------------ 28

General Quilting or Specialising -------------- 34

Your Start Up Needs ---------------------------- 35

   Your Sales pack ------------------------------------35

   Your Brochure -------------------------------------36

   Your Uniform --------------------------------------36

Starting Small With Your Premises ----------- 38

   Mall Karts and Kiosks ----------------------------38

   Market Stalls and Boot Fairs ---------------------41

Items You Will Need ---------------------------- 42

Quilting Basics ------------------------------------ 47

Finding Your Pattern ---------------------------- 50

Choosing And Preparing Fabric --------------- 51

How to Choose the Right Batting ------------- 54

The Art Of Appliquéing ------------------------- 57

Using Stencils ------------------------------------- 61

How to Use Templates in Quilting ------------ 63

Profitable New Quilting Business

Pricing Your Product ---------------------------- 65
Branding, Packaging And Other Stuff -------- 66
   Invoices and Order Forms ------------------------66
   Packaging --67
   Marketing Material----------------------------------67
   Website, store, kart, market stall -----------------67
Marketing Your Business --------------------- 68
   Sales packs --69
   Onsite Marketing -----------------------------------70
Administration ----------------------------------- 71
   Customer Administration---------------------------72
Your Customers --------------------------------- 74
   First Contact --------------------------------------74
   Estimating--76
Putting Your Business On The Internet ------ 79
   As A Shop Window---------------------------------79
   As A Full Site--------------------------------------80
   Factors To Remember ------------------------------81
An Internet Marketing Strategy -------------- 83
   Internet Advertising Kit ---------------------------84
   Internet Marketing Kit-----------------------------84
   Internet Marketing Tools --------------------------84
   Internet Marketing Strategy ----------------------85
Expanding -- 88
   Staff --88
   Advertising ---89

Profitable New Quilting Business

Customer Contracts --------------------------- 90
- Why Do I Need Contracts? ----------------------- 90
- Written and Verbal Contracts -------------------- 91
- Won't It Be Expensive? -------------------------- 92
- Contracts for Small Purchases. ------------------ 94

The Top 5 First-Year Mistakes --------------- 95
- Waiting for Customers to Come to You ---------- 95
- Spending Too Much on Advertising -------------- 96
- Being Too Nice ----------------------------------- 96
- Not Using the Phone ----------------------------- 97
- Hiring Professionals for Everything -------------- 98

Problems You May Have -------------------- 100

Time for a Holiday: But How? -------------- 101
- Tell People When You Are Going Away. -------- 101
- Change Your Voicemail Message. -------------- 102
- Set Up an Email Auto responder. -------------- 103
- Don't Stay Away Too Long. -------------------- 104
- Get Someone to Look after the Business. ------ 104

In Conclusion ------------------------------- 105

Quilting Terminology ----------------------- 106

Index --------------------------------------- 116

Legal Notice

We do not believe in get rich quick schemes. We do believe that business is equal parts of inspiration, hard work and luck. We ensure that every book that we sell will be interesting and useful to our clients. Every effort has been made to accurately represent our product and it's potential. Any testimonials and examples used are not intended to represent the average purchaser and are not intended to guarantee that anyone will achieve the same or similar results

Please remember that each individual's success depends on his or her background, dedication, desire, and motivation. As with any business endeavour, there is an inherent risk of loss of capital. **There is no guarantee that you will earn any money**.

Profitable New Quilting Business

This book will provide you with a number of suggestions you can use to better guarantee your chances for success. **We do not and cannot guarantee any level of profits.**

This product is written with the warning that any and every business venture contains risks, and any number of alternatives. We do not suggest that any one way is the right way or that our suggestions are the only way. On the contrary, we advise that before investing any money in a business venture you seek counselling and help from a qualified accountant and/or attorney.

**You read and use this book on the strict understanding that you alone are responsible for the success or failure of your business decisions relating to any information presented by our company
Biz Guru Ltd.**

Profitable New Quilting Business

Introduction

Quilting is a craft that has been around for centuries. For hundreds of years, the Chinese have used quilted cloth for their padded winter clothing. The Crusaders found that the quilted shirts worn by Arabs offered a great deal of protection under their chainmail. They even brought the idea back home in the 13th century. The process was adapted by European women for the use in creating bedcovers.

Quilting came to America with the Pilgrims, in the 16th century. Lack of resources made it necessary for the settlers to recycle their clothing and other fabrics; they made quilt tops, cutting the fabric into smaller pieces and patching or clouting it over and over until it wore out completely. These first quilts were more practical than pretty, but as the settlers prospered the designs became more colourful and elaborate. Appliqué also became a popular way of decorating the quilts and the patchwork quilt was officially born.

Profitable New Quilting Business

Around this time quilts became associated with the celebration of important events. Specific designs were created for specific reasons. The Double Wedding Ring design was used to mark a marriage or anniversary. This design was made from interlocking rings, each constructed from tiny patches. It was a very time consuming project, and usually was worked by multiple quilter's at the same time.

These days' patchwork quilts are traditionally made from scraps left over from past sewing projects. Not all scraps are suitable for this purpose. Loosely woven fabrics, such as muslin, are weak and prone to distortion, while very tightly woven fabrics, such as ticking, are not flexible enough and hard to stitch.

Cotton is the best fabric to use, especially for inexperienced quilters. Once a quilter is more experienced they may add other fabrics like silk, lightweight wool and so on.

Profitable New Quilting Business

The colour of a quilt is up to the creator. Most quilters plan their project carefully, or follow an established pattern. Making test patches is a great way to experiment. Colours are usually sorted into tones, light, medium and dark. Using tone helps to create depth and design. Textured fabric also creates different effects.

Quilting methods don't vary enormously throughout the world, but the designs are largely specific to a country, or a society and many designs have attracted worldwide favour.

Profitable New Quilting Business

Getting Your Business Started

Many people are thinking of starting a new business and quilting is certainly a popular choice. It is one of those businesses that you can start in a small way, providing you are able to obtain the necessary business licensing and certificates.

It is also a business that you can run quite easily from home with just a telephone and a simple filing system and obviously the appropriate equipment. You will need to ensure that you have a working room that is both clean and well equipped to a professional standard and some countries insist that you are regularly inspected.

It would also be advisable to have a background check if this is available. You should also obtain the appropriate insurance.

It would also be good to have at least two checkable references. Once you have all of these you should take photocopies and put them together as an sales pack.

Profitable New Quilting Business

If you have a good business plan, price your quiltings to make a profit and are good at time management, this can be a lucrative business.

Your main reason for wanting to start a quilting business should be that you are getting so many quilting orders that you feel you can go into business and make a go of it.

Profitable New Quilting Business

The Nasties

Tax, Insurance and Licences these are the nasties of your business and all of them are compulsory! Look up your local state/county/country web site to see what licences you will need. Similarly your country's tax web site will tell you what taxes you will need to pay, how you register to pay them and what forms you will need to fill in to become legal. Don't attempt to work without them – there goes the way to a world of misery. Tax officials in particular, are trained to find and collect unpaid taxes and these are always combined with extra costs and penalties.

Operating your business in some countries will require you and your staff to be licensed before you can start work. This should be displayed on your premises or available for view by your customers. You may also need a sales tax permit (USA and other sales tax based countries) or VAT registration (UK and some Europe and Asia) if you reach the VAT registration limit.

Will I Succeed?

You've got a great idea, you are pretty sure that what you have will sell; you've even got some cash together. Have you got what it will take to succeed? What else do you need?

Vision: You must be able to see where you are going and what the future will hold. See what others are not able to see and build your business on these visions.

Courage: The ability to act upon your vision despite having doubts. The readiness to give up job security and a planned future; for the chance of making a success with your new business. This takes courage.

Strategy: Having the courage to act upon your vision, you now need to build your strategies. You will need a business and a marketing strategy.

These are the formulas that you will use to drive forward and manage your business.

Profitable New Quilting Business

Planning Skills: To ensure that you reach your vision, you need copious amounts of planning. Planning how you will reach your targets, how you will meet new changes and challenges and how you will improve your business. You will need a business plan and a marketing plan.

Researching: Having decided what your business is going to be, then you will need to find out who will want to buy from your business and at what price. This takes a fair amount of researching.

Conceptualising: Knowing what you want to sell and to whom, you now need to define your products and services. Brainstorm different things that you associate with your company. Include everything, good and bad, until you are out of ideas.

Keep in mind that ideas generate ideas. Write everything down, this is how you move your company forward.

Profitable New Quilting Business

Use this period to design your products, what you want your company to look like and how you want it to be perceived by your customers.

Creativity: You will need the ability to think outside of the box. Keep ahead of your competitors by coming up with new, unusual and unique concepts and solutions to their needs. You will need to create marketing materials, packaging and sales pitches – all will need verbal and visual creativity.

Determination: Along the way you will come across many hurdles and set backs, you will need to dig deep, make your changes and keep going. Determination and the belief in your visions and plans will keep you on the road to success.

Humour: When the entire world seems against you and all seems to be going wrong, when your customers seem to be your worst enemy then you need a sense of humour to carry you forward.

Profitable New Quilting Business

A Successful Business Start up

Right you have sorted out your business ideas, you are ready to go ahead and you know what you want to sell and to whom. Now you need your business structure. These are all the things that make up your business. They include:

- **Legal Base:** This includes such factors as your licenses, insurances and setting up your company.
- **Your Market:** You need to decide who you want to market your services to and where they will be.
- **Your Services:** You now need to decide what services you are going to offer to these people, how you would like to package them and what prices you wish to charge.
- **Your Business Plan:** Whether you are looking for funding or not – a business plan is the foundation of a new business.
- **Your Funding:** You should now take your business plan and look around for funding, starting with your Bank.

Profitable New Quilting Business

- **Your Premises:** Look around for your new premises, preferably in the middle of your potential market. Remember that central to your success is the position you choose for your business. Foot traffic past your door and many potential customers within a short journey from your new business is vital to you finding customers.
- **Web Site:** Most businesses have them now – so even if you don't want to set one up now – at least buy and hold onto your domain name – in case someone else gets hold of it.
- **Your Staff:** Good staff that reflect your business ideals are vital so spend some time spend some time finding the best staff you can.
- **Marketing:** So important and so difficult to get right. Start with a good marketing strategy and go from there.
- **Grand Opening:** Make sure you make a splash and attract as much curiosity as possible.

Your Business Framework

When starting a business of what ever kind, large or small, there is a always a require framework or scaffolding that you have to set up. Not only does this make your business much more effective, but it also saves you from a lot of embarrassing and costly problems. When you start up your business, remember to tick off the 10 items below and you will have a very sound start to your business. Here is your framework:

- **Business Name.** Choose an appropriate name that sums up what your business stands for. It has to be unique – try and ensure that a suitable domain name is also available as you will probably want a web site as well. The owner of an established web site might cause problems if you give your brick based business the same name – so be careful in your choice.
- **Your Business Entity.** Obtain professional advice as whether to the best way to set up your business as a limited company, partnership etc. Then register your company.

- **Patents and Trademarks.** If you have unique products then you need to ensure that you have registered your patents before your start trading. Similarly any product names, mottos, selling tags etc should be trademarked. Take professional advice on how to do this.
- **Licenses and Permits.** Ensure that you have all the licenses and permits that you are legally required to have.
- **Insurance.** You may think that you don't need this but you do and will. So take out property, business, vehicle liability, staff and disaster insurance. A good broker can advise you.
- **Taxes.** A necessary evil I am afraid. Register with your local tax collector. Set up a good accounting system and hire a good accountant.
- **Employment Laws.** Establish what you local employment laws are and ensure that you adhere to them. Set up employee guidelines and handbooks. Make sure you hire and fire legally.

Profitable New Quilting Business

- **Banking.** Visit your local banks and find the best business bank account and credit card for you business. Always keep your business and personal spending separate.
- **Business Plan.** This is your carefully written plan on how you want your company to operate, what you want to sell, where and to whom. It includes your business and marketing strategy as well as your financial standing and projections. This is the foundation of your business.
- **Liquid Cash.** Ensure that you have enough money to carry your through the first few months of your business as well as any foreseeable troublesome times ahead.

Profitable New Quilting Business

How Much Does It Cost To Start A Business?

You've got your business idea, think that you will be able to get a good loan and even have your business plan being written but…. The one big burning issue is – How much does it cost to start a business?

Well you first of all have to be realistic and understand that you are unlikely to make a profit within the first six months of business – so you should also budget for your first six months running costs. So here is your shopping list:

1. **Purchase of lease/franchise.** This will include any Realtor fees, deposits and other legal expenses. Even party sellers need some kind of premises. To start with you can use a home office, but you are going to need somewhere to hold all that stock and marketing materials that you will soon need.

Profitable New Quilting Business

2. **Cost of fit out and purchase of new equipment.** This will include any work that needs to be done on your premises as well as any equipment you have to buy in order to start and run your business. Often you can lease equipment in order to mitigate high start up costs. This also includes a car or van to deliver your stock to your distributors.

3. **Six months worth of advertising and marketing.** This will be particularly high at the start as you establish your business. Factor in some cold calling as well as a launch party or opening day. Marketing will include a lot of local advertising in order to attract good distributors.

4. **Legal, licensing and banking costs.** Your business will need to be set up correctly, licensed and have a good bank account. Sadly all of these require money. You may also need a payment processing service to use credit cards.

5. **Staff costs for six months.** Staff will be the basis of providing good service to your new customers. Make sure that you have enough money put aside to find them, train them and keep them! Much of your staff costs will be on a commission basis but you will still require admin staff and one or two "on staff" distributors and maybe warehouse staff as well. They will all want to be paid, often before you get paid for your sales.

6. **Uniforms, office and marketing supplies, packaging etc.** You will need to establish your brand. This means that your staff will need uniforms or at the least business cards and name tags. You will need brochures, adverts etc. If appropriate you will also need standardized packaging and documentation. Your office will also need office equipment and supplies. You should also budget for designing your logo, brochures and adverts if you cannot do this yourself.

7. **Stock and supplies** – to keep you going for six months.

Profitable New Quilting Business

8. **Maintenance for six months** – your equipment will also need to keep going for six months. This includes your cars, computers, printers, copiers etc. Budget for a lot of printing ink!
9. **Any loans that you have will also have to be paid.** Again look at least at six months or until you break even and can pay the loan.
10. **Your salary for six months** – lastly you will need to pay your own bills and maintain your family during this time. You should expect that for a short while your standard of living will go down.

Add this up and add 10% for contingency and some good luck.

Common Business Mistakes.

All entrepreneurs have to learn from their own mistakes as they build their business, but wouldn't it be great to have some one tell you what the common mistakes are and how to avoid them? You Want a Successful Business – So Don't Do This!

- **Believing that you will start earning straight away.** All businesses take time to establish themselves – even internet based ones. People need to know where you are, what you sell and most importantly, that they can trust your company to deliver what it promises. Expect to spend at least 6 months working away at your business before you break even – sometimes longer.
- **Believing in Get Rich Quick Schemes:** A good business is established by part inspiration, part perspiration and just a little bit of luck!

Profitable New Quilting Business

- **Believing that you can set up a business and it continually earns for you.** Even a very profitable business needs continual management to ensure that your profit does not erode. Your products and marketing need to continually change to meet the changing circumstances in the real world.
- **Believing that you can earn whilst you are aware from the office.** Even if you fully automate your business and hire really good staff, there is always an element of "while the cat is away". That is why there are so many "absent owner" sales.
- **Being a single product company.** As good as your product may be, markets and tastes will change and so must you. If your product is very good – other companies will quickly take action to seize your market share by bringing in similar products at cheaper prices.

- **Not offering upgrades and enhancements.** It is far easier and cheaper to sell to existing customers. You do this by offering upgrades and enhancements to their existing products. You should have a group of products at several increasing price points.
- **Relaxing after you success.** Businesses need continual effort, management and improvements. Although a product launch is hard work, you should start on your next product shortly afterwards. This will give you sustainable success and several income streams.
- **Believing that a business can be established with little capital.** Marketing, infrastructure purchases, stock, advertising and staff all cost money and must be purchased in order to make a profit. Cash flow kills more business than anything else.

- **Believing that you know all you have to.** Your competitors may have been in the business longer than you have, your customers may be very knowledgeable. Meeting customer needs is a constantly changing landscape and you need to keep up to date on the latest trends and technology. You need to be able to project yourself as an expert in the field you work in. If you do not have this knowledge then learn it or buy it in!
- **Not investing in your staff.** Your staff are the public face of your business. They should be well trained, knowledgeable and well dressed as well as fully motivated to sell on your behalf.
- **Not motivating** your staff. Good staff are hard to find and difficult to keep. Good staff help your business expand and be profitable. Good staff will grow your business exponentially as word of mouth spreads so you must look after them or you may find them working directly for your client.

Profitable New Quilting Business

- **Not motivating** your distributors or sales staff sufficiently. Selling on commission only is very hard work, it must be rewarding and your staff should feel that they will benefit from it. Your distributors, particularly at the beginning will be chasing around looking for retail outlets, doing a lot of mileage, delivering stock and looking after retailers. So they need motivating and reward well. Good distributors will grow your business exponentially so you must look after them.
- **Distribution problems.** Once you get established, the geographic area you are selling to becomes larger. Care must be taken that you can get your goods to your new customers. The cost of mailing and delivering your items must be properly calculated and included in the sales price.

Profitable New Quilting Business

- **Stock Holdings.** With distribution problems comes stock holding problems, the more products you have, the more stock you must have. If you have different sizes and colours this figure goes up even more! It is very important that you work out how much stock you need as stock is dead money hold no more and no less!
- **Branding.** It is important that your company is recognised and has a good image. This helps spread the word about your services! Otherwise why would your customers hire you? Spend on your brand, it's worth it!

Learn these lessons well, avoid the mistakes at all costs you should save valuable time and resources by doing things right the first time. Good luck.

Profitable New Quilting Business

General Quilting or Specialising

There are many types of quilting. You might want to be a generalist or you might want to specialise in one kind of quilt or one style. Some ideas you might want to look at are:

- **Celebration Quilts:** birth, marriage, engagement, Christmas, Easter, Golden Weddings etc.
- **Presents:** birthday, grandparents, grandchildren, vacation etc.
- **Geographic:** quilts make great souvenirs.
- **Club or Society:** sports clubs, Brownies, W.I. etc.

You might also look at different styles of quilt, different types of quilt or even niche areas such as pets pictures, fantasy etc. You could even produce just pet quilts or cushions!

To be general gets you a potentially bigger audience, but niche selling gets you more loyalty.

Profitable New Quilting Business

Your Start Up Needs

There are a few things that you will need on your start up. These will make you look professional and help you market your business.

Your Sales pack

The sales packet is the major step in the Quilting business – it is what makes your business professional. The sales packet must contain a printout or photocopy of your terms and conditions, insurance and background check, references and your brochure.

In your terms and conditions you should explain the details of your working policy. This will give information such as: your hours of operation; when a deposit and full payment is due; if you will deliver or not etc. All these details should be included in your terms and conditions in order to not only look organised and professional but also to avoid misunderstandings in the future.

Profitable New Quilting Business

Your Brochure

Your brochure can be quickly made up on a PC. Design a one page description of your business and the kind of work that you do. Include your contact details and company name. Do not include too many words – just make it catchy, memorable and informative. You can include a couple of graphics which you can easily find on the internet.

If you wish you can also include a business card. These can be professionally produced from web sites such as vistaprint or from you local stationary store or printer. Now you have your sales pack.

Your Uniform

It would also be a good idea to give yourself some kind of uniform. You can buy smart coveralls from large department stores or uniform stores or you get t shirts or sweaters printed with your company name. Visit CafePress for some ideas.

Profitable New Quilting Business

Match your colours of your uniform and your equipment to your company colours. This makes you look like a professional company. Make sure that everything is cleaned regularly – including your equipment so that you are always ready to work and look professional to your customers.

Profitable New Quilting Business

Starting Small With Your Premises

Sometimes circumstances dictate that you can't afford a retail shop but you really want to get your business started. Many small, retail businesses are not suitable to run from your home base or via a warehouse. Web sites, whilst having low start up costs, also take a lot of marketing and time to become profitable. Why not think about starting a kart or kiosk in a shopping mall? Here are a few points to consider.

Mall Karts and Kiosks

As always Location, Location, Location: The location of your business is crucial to its survival. A store's location can often spell its success or failure. Without sufficient store recognition, a business can suffer poor cash flow and will inevitably fail over time. Your business needs to be physically located out in midst of everyday life, in broad daylight where shoppers can easily find you.

Profitable New Quilting Business

The location itself of the mall plays a huge role in your kart's success. Is the mall located in an isolated part of the city or town, or right in the heart of the action? You must forecast the level as well as the timing of traffic your business will receive during the morning, midday, and late afternoon on each day of the week. Therefore, you can efficiently establish an employment schedule as well as appropriate operating hours.

Choose your mall carefully so that it has ample traffic of potential customers. Go there with a "clicker" and see how many people pass by per hour. Visit on several different days of the week as well as at different times.

Quality of Traffic: It is one thing to have steady traffic, and another to have the kind of traffic that your business needs. Some malls attract low-to-middle income people; others are targeted towards the upper class. Choose wisely.

Profitable New Quilting Business

Position in the Mall: Your success in a mall will depend on whether you are located in a section that is conducive to what your business is selling. You should look at the **complementary nature of the adjacent stores.** If you are a gourmet store, you may want to be located near a restaurant where people are already in their "hunger fulfilling" state of mind. Complementary businesses, such as fine jewellery and gourmet food, have also been proven to work well together as both its customers are likely to have disposable income and a tendency to spend for these two genres of luxury products.

Similarly **high volume areas** where lines of patrons form, such as theatres or department stores, are also good mall locations as it could give potential customers several minutes to look in your display or listen to your sales pitch.

Profitable New Quilting Business

Costs: Rental costs in shopping malls are often higher than rates in downtown Main Street. You main consideration should be: will the higher traffic compensate for the increased rental cost?

If you can easily recover your monthly rental payment and overhead expenses, you're in a good position to make a profit.

People Buy with their Eyes! Lastly ensure that you display your products in an tempting manner. Karts and Kiosks are very good in selling items that are "impulse buys". Make your products appealing and your sales pitch interesting and your sales will increase!

Market Stalls and Boot Fairs

The same criteria about location appertains to market stalls and boot fairs. Obviously your outlay will be much smaller – but so will your potential income. Care should be taken to ensure that your stall looks professional and well branded otherwise your business will be classed as a "hobby business" and people will expect to pay correspondingly low prices.

Profitable New Quilting Business

Items You Will Need

Quilting is quite a low cost business to start up but you will need some equipment to make your work easier. Start with a sewing machine, the most basic of your supplies. Though it is technically possible to sew a quilt without a machine, and some people still prefer to do it, most busy crafters today like to use a machine. You'll want to at least use it for piecing together the blocks for the quilt top, and after that you can choose to do the actual quilting by hand or machine. But most quilters would agree that the sewing machine is the most essential of your supplies, and so the soundest advice is to buy the best you can afford. You will also need:

- **Metal-edged ruler and tape measures** - used when creating templates and cutting cardboard and fabric with a rotary cutter or knife. Also used with set squares to cut lengths of fabric.
- **Vanishing markers** to create special marks that will fade in contact with water.
- **Dressmaker's wheels and chalk** to directly mark fabric.

Profitable New Quilting Business

- **Scissors,** Dressmaker's scissors and shears used for cutting fabric only. Paper scissors and embroidery scissors.
- **Pinking shears** have serrated blades. They are used to create decorative edges and prevent fraying.
- **Rotary cutters** are used with a cutting mat. They are great for cutting multiple pieces that are exactly the same, at the same time. Rotary cutters are available in different sizes. Small cutters work best for cutting curves and a few layers of fabric. Large cutters cut many layers at a time and are ideal for cutting long straight lines.
- **Cutting mats** are made especially for use with rotary cutters. They protect both the tabletop and the blade. Mats with printed grids are useful for cutting right angles.
- **Quilter's needles** are used for hand sewing appliqué and patchwork. Betweens are used for making smaller stitches.
- **Crewel needles** are used for working embroidery stitches.
- **Quilting pins** are longer than dressmaker's pins and pass through several layers of fabric easily.

- **Safety pins** are sometimes used in basting quilt blocks together.
- **Beeswax** is applied to quilting thread before stitching so that the thread passes smoothly through the fabric.
- **Thimbles** are essential for hand quilting. They are used to push the needle through several layers of fabric at once.
- **Unpickers**-or rippers are used to remove stitches.
- **Iron,** used for pressing patchwork seams and to remove wrinkles from fabric.
- **Embroidery hoops** are used while quilting. Wooden frames are usually used for hand quilting. Plastic frames with metal spring closures are used for machine quilting.
- **Quilters'** gloves offer protection when using rotary cutters and needles.
- **Needle threaders** make threading needles a breeze.

Profitable New Quilting Business

As well as fabric pieces for your quilts you will need:

- **Padding** for the centre of your quilt.
- **Ribbon** may be used to embellish appliqué or crazy patchwork. It may also be used to edge a border. Ribbon may be velvet, satin or man made material.
- **Trimmings** such as fringing, pompon tape; tassels and flat ribbon tape may be used to make unusual edgings or to embellish a patchwork piece.
- **Lace** can be used to embellish appliqués.
- **Thread** in multiple colours to match your materials.
- **Patterns** that make designing and sewing your quilt that much quicker. More in the next chapter.

Profitable New Quilting Business

In your office you will need:

- **PC and printer** for research, pattern making and business administration.
- **Mood board** to use to design your next quilt.
- **Idea board** to be placed near your sewing machine used as a place to pin swatches, arrange fabrics in potential colour combinations, and post ideas torn from magazines.
- **Digital camera** to take quality pictures of your quilts for marketing purposes.

Quilting Basics

Quilts are made of three layers. The top piece is the layer that is decorated and most elaborate. The middle piece is a layer of batting, or wadding that provides warmth. The third piece is the backing. These three layers are held together with lines of stitching. These lines may be worked in a grid, in straight rows or elaborate patterns. Originally they were sewn by hand with a needle. Today some quilters still produce quilts this way, while others prefer machine quilting.

Pre-wash all fabrics in mild detergent and warm water before starting a quilt. Any fabrics that may run should be washed separately. When the fabrics are dry they should be ironed, either with a steam iron, or a dry iron and a clean damp cloth.

In the pioneer days the only equipment needed to produce a quilt included a needle, thread and material, and hopefully a pair if shears and a thimble.

A wooden frame would be constructed to allow the quilter to use both hands, or to enable more than one sewer to work at a time.

Quilting bees were popular social gatherings. Today many quilters prefer to use a large wooden hoop to make their projects more portable.

Patterns can be made from almost anything. The traditional American patterns work on a block or section, and are repeated throughout the quilt, with each block being made up of a number of pieces. The quilts are then edged to surround the blocks.

For patchwork quilting – most American Colonial Style for example, it's very straight forward to make your patterns, and you can find lots of examples, with sizes, for you to print off from the internet.

Profitable New Quilting Business

Cut paper templates for your shapes, and then trace them on to sand paper (fine gauge) or plastic template material. Then trace the templates onto the fabric and cut out.

If you are making a quilt from varying shaped pieces, you can make a large paper or card design, and gradually cut out and put together sections to match your design.

Finding Your Pattern

Free patterns abound on the internet, as do patterns for purchase. Individual patterns are available for various quilt blocks. If you know what quilt you want to make, it can be a good idea to purchase one of these, as it will have detailed directions on every aspect of the specific block. You'll find step-by-step directions that cover every aspect of the pattern for your quilt. The pattern may also give you tips and techniques you wouldn't otherwise know.

Another excellent source for patterns is to visit your library or the bookstore and peruse the quilting section, where you'll see pattern book after pattern book. These books can be especially valuable if you haven't yet decided on a certain quilt pattern. With a little research, it's easy to find the perfect pattern for your quilting needs as well as some ideas for future projects.

Choosing And Preparing Fabric

Choosing fabric for a quilting project can be as much fun as preparing the quilt itself. Different fabrics will make each quilt unique. Most quilter's prefer using fabric that is 100 % cotton because they are easier to sew, mark, press and hand quilt. If you are shopping for fabric in a quilt shop you will rarely find fabric that is not pure cotton. Fabrics will also probably be arranged according to colours and print types.

With more experience fabrics other than cotton may be added for variety. Not all fabrics are suitable however. If you are using an unusual fabric for the first time, or want to use different types of fabrics together, try a small test block first. Fabrics of a medium density, with an even weave work well. Loosely woven fabrics are prone to distortion, as are stretch fabrics. Silk, lightweight wool and some plastics may be used with experience.

Both the colour and tone of the fabric you choose will influence the overall effect of the pattern that you choose. Tone may be used to create depth and interest with greater effect than when using colour alone. Good planning is necessary to achieve the desired look.

Colour is greatly affected by the colours around it. Using contrasting colours will make pieces of a quilt block stand out from each other. Combing certain warm colours such as reds, yellows and oranges, in the same quilt block as cool colours like blues, greens or violets, will make them look more vivid.

Combining fabrics with various print scales and styles can add visual texture to your quilt. Interesting visual effects may also be achieved by using colours of graduated values. Printed cotton fabrics are available in many designs and styles including batiks, homespun plaids and florals, tiny-grained prints that look like solids, reproduction prints, and soft flannels.

Profitable New Quilting Business

Quilt blocks made from fabrics of the same or various shades of one colour, but of contrasting textures can create pleasing results. Fabrics with a nap such as velvet, or fabrics with sheen like taffeta also provide interest.

Whatever fabric you choose for your quilting project, you must prepare it properly before you begin. Most cotton fabrics shrink when they are washed and dried. If you do not preshrink your fabric before you make your quilt, the fabrics may pucker at the stitching lines and the finished product may shrink in size the first time it is washed.

To prevent this wash all fabrics first in a washing machine on a short gentle cycle. Machine dry the fabric and press it with an iron. You are now ready to begin your quilt.

How to Choose the Right Batting

The correct batting for their quilting projects, but it can make the difference between a successful quilting project and an unsuccessful one. The right batting can have an enormous effect on the finished appearance of your quilting project. It can also make the difference between enjoying the process of quilting or hating it. You spend hours planning the design and look of the outer layers of your quilting project, why not take the time to learn a bit about the batting that goes inside?

Batting is the insulating fabric, which is the part of the quilt that creates warmth. Batting is layered between the quilt top and the backing. This quilting sandwich of three layers of fabric is then pinned at the edges in order to temporarily secure it. Most commonly it is then sewn together, either by hand or machine, but sometimes crafters tie the layers of batting and fabric together.

Profitable New Quilting Business

Usually yarn is used to tie a quilting project together, but sometimes several strands of thread are used also. Be certain to tie a tight square knot if you choose this method of securing the batting to the fabric. You want to be sure the quilt will stand up to years of use.

Batting comes in several different fibres, most often polyester, cotton, and wool. Polyester batting has a high loft which will remain through repeated washings. It is generally hypo-allergenic and usable for either hand or machine quilting projects.

Cotton batting is a quilter's dream. It has a much lower loft than the polyester batting, and is often used when quilters want to achieve an antique look. As cotton is a natural fibber, it "breathes," meaning it will help you to remain cool in the summer and warm in the winter. Cotton batting is not as suitable for tying, as it has a tendency to clump. Like cotton, wool batting breathes.

Profitable New Quilting Business

There are two different ways batting is manufactured—needle punched or bonded. Needle punched batting is a good utilitarian choice for a quilting project that needs to stand up to hard use. It is made by thousands of needles piercing the batting, interlocking the fibres. The needle punched batting is firmer and heavier than bonded batting, which is manufactured by using a bonding agent to adhere the layers of the batting together.

Many battings, whatever form you choose, are available either pre-cut or rolled on a tube so that you can cut your own to size. If your quilting project is a standard quilt size you will probably be able to find a pre-cut batting quite easily. For other sizes you may need to buy batting on the roll.

The Art Of Appliquéing

Appliqué is a quilting technique which involves applying layering one fabric above another and sewing it on. The term appliqué comes from the French word appliquer, which is a French verb meaning "to put on." Even though the word comes from the French, the technique has been used in many cultures and throughout history, with the earliest examples of appliqué being found thousands of years ago. Learning the uses and how-tos of appliqué will expand the possibilities of quilting enormously for you. Appliqué is a versatile technique which is useful for design options regular quilting can't accomplish.

The first step in learning appliqué is selecting a design. Small, intricate shapes will not work well for this technique, at least not when you are first learning.

Profitable New Quilting Business

Start with a simple shape for your beginning appliqué project. Something basic like a circle or heart will serve you well for your first attempt. In order to create a pattern for your appliqué design, many people choose freezer paper, because it is stiff without being too thick. Trace your design onto the freezer paper and cut it out and then you can easily trace your appliqué onto the fabric you've selected cotton is a good choice). Next, carefully cut the appliqué design out, leaving 1/8th inches all around.

In order to stabilise the appliqué, you can either glue the freezer paper to the fabric design, or pin it. Now you will have to deal with the raw edges. Since the fabrics are being layered atop one another, as opposed to being sewn in seams as with traditional quilting, it's very important to learn to finish the raw edges so they won't unravel and be unsightly.

Profitable New Quilting Business

One way to do this is to take your scissors and carefully snip to the marked line and then press the seam allowance under all the way around your design. Use the tip of a Popsicle stick or a chopstick to help smooth the little edges of fabric down.

Now position the appliqué design where you want it on the base fabric and hand stitch it down. There are several possibilities for stitching your appliqué. Do you want to hide the stitches or use it as a decorative element for your appliqué? If you want to hide the stitching, blind stitch or hem stitch are good possibilities. For decorative touches, try buttonhole stitching. You can use any embroidery stitch that strikes your fancy, but with some of the more complicated stitches it's a good idea to anchor your appliqué with a hem stitch first.

Profitable New Quilting Business

The last step is to very carefully cut a small slit in the background fabric only, behind the appliqué. Be certain not to cut through the appliqué itself! Then gently reach in and remove the freezer paper. Now turn your appliqué over and press it, smoothing the edges and taking care if you've used a decorative embroidery stitch. That's it! That's how easy it is to learn to appliqué. Once you've tried your hand at appliqué, you will be glad you've added it to your quilting repertoire.

Using Stencils

Stencils are actually very useful in the art of quilting and advances in technology are quickly making them a must-have tool. Quilting stencils are very similar to stencils for paint, and often look about the same. They are most often made from a sturdy plastic, with holes punched in it for the design. They are used to lay down a pattern to follow when stitching. The use of quilting stencils allows quilters to reproduce elaborate patterns on their quilt tops. With quilting stencils, you have an easy way to transfer and then follow a stitching design.

Many companies offer quilting stencils and the supplies you'll need to go with them. You'll find designs ranging from traditional florals and fans to very contemporary styles. Take a look around some of the quilting sites on the internet or visit your local quilting store to get an idea of how many stencils await you.

Profitable New Quilting Business

Quilting stencils are easy to use. To transfer the design you can use chalk or stitching or water-soluble pens. All you have to do is lay the quilting stencil atop your fabric and trace the pattern. Voila! You now have a stitching pattern to follow without a lot of muss and fuss. A simple rule of thumb is to choose a design about a half an inch to an inch smaller than your block, so that the resulting pattern doesn't look crowded. You can also take one of the smaller stencils and repeat the design by laying it down in a pattern on your fabric.

How to Use Templates in Quilting

Usually made from sturdy clear acrylic, and designed to be used over and over again, templates make marking and cutting pieces for a quilt block a breeze.

Templates generally have seam line and other markings on them for the convenience of quilters. The best templates are laser cut to ensure exact precision for measurement. With quilting templates, a rotary cutter, and a mat, you can cut the pieces for numerous blocks at one time

Quilting templates are available in every size and shape imaginable. Every geometric shape is represented, and you can buy a set of basic templates for squares and circles and rectangles so you always have them on hand. You can also buy sets of templates for a specific quilt block.

Profitable New Quilting Business

The process is simple-lay your neatly ironed fabric on the rotary mat, place the acrylic template atop it, hold it firmly and use the rotary cutter to trim around the edges.

Once you get the hang of it, you can cut several layers of fabric at once. Using templates, you can spend an hour or two cutting pieces for quilt blocks, and get to the actual sewing and quilting so much faster.

Quilters may also want to take the time to browse the web or go to the library or local bookstore for books. Many quilting sites and books contain useful information about using templates, with tips and techniques listed that will make the process even easier. The quilting sites contain are often also laden with photos showing the use of templates in a step-by-step manner, which can be very helpful. Although the process of using templates is simple, there are always trade secrets that can make it even easier.

Profitable New Quilting Business

Pricing Your Product

Pricing is so important to the success of your business. When pricing your quilt look at the following:

- Cost of the materials.
- Fuel costs to make the quilt.
- A percentage of your equipment costs.
- Cost of your time.
- Delivery costs.
- Packaging costs.

You should set some money aside to build up your brand image by advertising and training your staff. People are more likely to come to you if they know your product.

Now have a look at what other quilters are charging and try and ensure your prices are similar.

By managing your stock levels to an optimum level, you should be able to keep the costs to a minimum.

Branding, Packaging And Other Stuff

Branding is so important. It is how people recognise your company and what you are selling. People will more readily hold parties for companies that they recognise and buy products that understand and know.

Your brand is so much more than your logo; it is your company name, your web site and the colours that you use. Everything that your customers and staff see should be "stamped" with your company brand and be instantly recognised as belonging to your company. So let us look at where your will be using your brand.

Invoices and Order Forms

They should have your company details, contact details and web site as well as your logo.

Profitable New Quilting Business

Packaging

It stands to reason that all your packaging, including that used in delivering your items, should be stamped with your company name, logo, phone number and web site. All packaging should include further Order Forms and a catalogue.

Marketing Material

Once again you should market such that your company and how to contact it, is instantly recognisable. How and where you advertise should also back up your brand image. If you are selling family friendly items then you would not advertise in a "lad's mag" for example.

Website, store, kart, market stall

However you sell your goods, they must have your logo and contact details emblazoned over them as well as completely reflecting your brand.

Profitable New Quilting Business

Marketing Your Business

The first thing you need to do is contact your friends and neighbours and see if they need your services or know someone who does.

Now set up an advert on your PC. You can print them off, on postcards quite easily. It should read something like this.

Quilting

Quilts for births, celebrations and weddings

For more details,

Call CompanyX: 123-4567 - ABC Quilts

In essence, you have a professional advertising "billboard." Now is the time to use a bit of shoe leather. Put the cards on notice boards in supermarkets, shops, clubs, offices etc. Always ask first. You can also put a similar advert in your local papers if that is affordable.

Profitable New Quilting Business

If you also decided to use business cards – use the front to put your company name, contact details and a one line description of your services. On the back put your short advert. Leave these wherever you are allowed to and concentrate on where you will find your potential clients.

It takes a short while to start up any kind of company. Start touting for small contracts to begin with particularly those that you can do yourself. As you get more work or get offered larger contracts you can start to consider taking on staff.

Sales packs

Set up an sales pack. It should be quite small – say A4 or A5 and a few pages. Include details of your company and products as well as a few sample designs, your prices and some great photos of quilts you have done. Include some references if you have them.

This will be given to prospective customers who are seeking to purchase bespoke or customised quilts.

Onsite Marketing

Whichever retail outlet you chose, ensure that you have plenty of brochures available to give out to interested potential customers. Don't leave them on the counter otherwise you will go through a lot of them for little return – save them for the really interested people. You could leave business cards for anyone to take- people tend to take these only if they are interested. You should display some good samples as well as a lot of items for sale. Be prepared to take orders from your stall.

Administration

Administration is very important. Without good administration your company will quickly disintegrate into chaos and you won't know who has what and who needs to pay for services and who needs them to be cleaned and when. Your administration should include ways of controlling or managing the following:

- Collecting money from your customers
- Banking money.
- Managing enquiries and complaints.
- Invoice and bill payment.
- Accounts and book keeping including, payroll, banking, taxes and VAT/taxes.
- Purchasing and auditing equipment. At least once a year and preferably quarterly, equipment must be checked against your accounts and for the need to be repaired.
- Salary and commission payments.
- Staff training and development.

Profitable New Quilting Business

It may seem a lot, but if you start small and get yourself a good accounts package, a good accountant and bank manager it is a lot easier.

Customer Administration

- Set up a file for each of your customers with their contact details, what you have agreed to do, the price to be charged and any other details. Keep a folder/file for each customer. Add each order to the file – latest order on top. The file should include all contact details. If you have a number of orders per client put a list of orders on top and tick them off as you complete them. If you have a lot of customers have a customer number format.
- You should also keep a record of money due and paid. You should be able to find a good accounting system very easily. Always give a receipt.
- Make a To-Do list of all your orders and tick off those that have been completed. Put in order of importance/when delivered.

Profitable New Quilting Business

- Keep a detailed diary of when they have to be delivered by. In the diary also note what extra services were requested and what payment you need for the service.
- Keep a diary of what money is due when and by who – refer to it each day and chase that money! Keep invoices separate to use for your accounts and to keep track of what you are owed.

Your Customers

Once you spread the word that you're in the business of quilting you'll have no trouble at all keeping busy!

When prospective clients call or email you, explain your services and prices. With this kind of service it is best to either ask for a 50% deposit or a 100% payment. This is because once you have finished the service; it is sometimes hard to obtain the payment due. Make sure that you receive all the payment due before you finish the service.

First Contact

When a prospective customer calls, have your appointment book and a pen handy. Be friendly and enthusiastic. Explain what you do and offer to show a few samples.

Profitable New Quilting Business

When they ask how much you charge, simply give them a wide range and say that you will give a firm cost quote, once you've discussed their requirements. Then without much of a pause, ask if 4:30 this afternoon would be convenient for them, or if 5:30 would be better.

You must pointedly ask if they can come to make your cost proposal at a certain time, or the decision may be put off, and you may come up with a "no sale." You may prefer to visit them if you do not have a suitable reception area.

Just as soon as you have an agreement on the time and place to make you cost proposal and marked it in your appointment book, ask for their name, address and telephone number.

Jot this information down on a 3 by 5 card, along with the date and the notation: Prospective Customer. Then you file this card in a permanent card file.

Save these cards, because there are literally hundreds of ways to turn this prospect file into real cash, once you've accumulated a sizeable number of names, addresses and phone numbers.

Estimating

When you go to see your prospect in person, always be on time. A couple of minutes early won't hurt you, but a few minutes late will definitely be detrimental to your closing the sale. If they are coming to you then ensure that you give good directions and are ready for them.

Always be well groomed. Dress as a successful business owner. Be confident and sure of yourself; be knowledgeable about what you can do as well as understanding of the prospect's needs and wants. Do not smoke, even if invited by the prospect, and never accept a drink - even coffee - until after you have a signed contract in your briefcase. It's important to appear methodical, thorough and professional

A little small talk after the sale is appropriate, but becoming too friendly is not. You create an impression, and preserve it, by maintaining a business-like relation ship.

When you go to make your cost estimate, take along a ruled tablet on a clipboard a calculator, your appointment book and your list of sample designs.

You should also have at least two of your sales packs (one for the customer and the rest for her friends that may also need your services) and a blank contract (more of this later). A receipt book would also be a good idea. You can buy folios in stationary stores that will keep these all tidy.

If they choose one of your sample designs, fine, but if they want a particular design of their own, now is the time to ask for photos or start jotting down all their requirements, including sizes and colours.

Profitable New Quilting Business

You should hopefully come up with a drawing of what they require in front of them. Get them to sign off these details and picture so that there is no dispute later. You will probably have to come back to them with a firm price. Make sure that it is possible for you to actually produce this quilt!

Discuss when they need the quilt and if you are delivering the quilt of if they are collecting it from you.

Now complete the contract for them, summarizing what you have just agreed and confirm that you will send her a typed up list of all the quilt decoration details you have just completed. Ask them for confirmation on the contract and for a deposit if applicable. Also offer them an sales pack for their friend who may need your services.

Congratulations you have just made a sale!

Putting Your Business On The Internet

Just about anyone can put a web site up on the internet and now days it is quite easy. You have two choices as how to set up your website:
- As a shop window for your company, with contact details etc.
- As a fully working site with ecommerce facilities.

Which ever option you choose, you first need a god domain name. Go to a good domain provider like enom, Godaddy, namecheap NOT registerfly and spend under £10 on a domain. Choose a domain name that has the word dating, love etc in it. This will help with your search engine positioning as well as act as a memory jog to your potential customers.

As A Shop Window

Hop over to hostgator or similar and then buy a monthly hosting account. With that will come a site maker - where you can easily set up a web site using one of thousands of templates. You can add payment processor linkages, forums etc.

Profitable New Quilting Business

The only problem you will have is you want to sell promote or talk about illegal activities, terrorist activities or sex or have a high usage activity such as Myspace etc.

As A Full Site

You will probably need to get this especially written and designed for you. Put your project on sites like guru/elance/scriptlance etc and find a competitive quote.

Get yourself a PayPal account or similar so that you can take payment on your web site. This is much more secure and quicker than taking checks.

Profitable New Quilting Business

Factors To Remember

Always consider your target market when designing your web site. Include some helpful information about your subject matter but nothing that will give away what you are trying to sell!

Ensure that your contact details can be freely found and that details of your company and services are clearly set out.

As you will be asking for money before you deliver something – make your potential customer feel comfortable making payment and tell them what will happen next.

Respond to all enquiries and purchases very quickly. If this is difficult then set up an autoresponder to confirm you have received their enquiry/payment and will get back to them within a few hours.

Place references that you have received from past customers to show that you are a professional company.

Your challenge will be to be listed in the major search engines and then get traffic. Now market your web site like mad. It will take several months to make an impact in the major search engines. So build up your local custom whilst you are doing this. www.GetIntoGoogleFast.com – Does exactly what is says in the domain!

An Internet Marketing Strategy

Ok, you've got your web site set up, you are sure that it is search engine friendly and you are pretty certain what your customers want. You've identified at least 3 products that you want to promote and you think that they meet your potential customer's needs. So now what?

Well unfortunately the days, that I can remember, of "build it and they will come" have long gone. Unless you promote your web site – no one will know that you are there and no visitors means no sales. So where so you go from here? Well take a deep breath, a pen and paper and let's start on your Marketing Strategy. Briefly for a new business, with a relatively inexperienced marketer, your strategy will probably include the following options:

- Pay Per Click Advertising
- Article Marketing
- Email Marketing
- Community Marketing
- Classified Advertising

Profitable New Quilting Business

So let's get started – and before you start panicking, you are just writing your Marketing Strategy. This chapter will explain how to do all of the following.

Internet Advertising Kit

For each of your programs/products
- Write a short advert – say 50 words.
- Write a very short advert – say 15 words
- Write a short article – say about 400 – 600 words.
- Decide on your keywords – say about 30 – 50 words.

Internet Marketing Kit

For your web site theme
- Write at least 6 short auto responder messages.
- Find or write at least 2 giveaway products.

Internet Marketing Tools

- Your web site
- An autoresponder
- A good email account

Internet Marketing Strategy

Now let's put all of these together into your first Marketing Strategy.

- **Submit your web site to all the major search engines.** This will start to get your web site noticed. As this takes a long time, it needs to be the first thing that you do. You can do this yourself or pay someone else to do this for you. We provide this service for our customers for £20 a month, which includes submission to Google, Yahoo and MSN.

- **Set up your autoresponder form** on your web site and load your messages into the autoresponder. Ensure that you offer one of the giveaway products as a bonus for signing onto your ezine. The second giveaway can be set up for message 3 or 4. Your messages should be sent in the following intervals. Day 1,3,7,7,7,7

- **Set up your download pages**, for your bonus products as well as the products you are selling. Ensure that you provide an extra offer on each download page.

- **Submit your article** – including your resource box, to about 6 major ezine article sites. Limit yourself to 6 at the moment. Each of these submissions, if accepted will give you a link to your web site. If too many links to your new web site appear very quickly, search engines assume that you have been using "black hat" SEO tactics (a total no no) and will not list your site.
- **Identify 4 forums** that discuss the topics of your web site. Set yourself up an account name that describes you well. We use the name "Biz Guru" which is our trade mark and name. Set up your signature to include your web site address. You now have 4 good links to your web site.
- **Set up some classified ads**. You can do this one of two ways: i) choose one or two major sites/email lists and advertise with them. ii) use an ezine ad blaster to send your ad out to numerous lower quality places.

Profitable New Quilting Business

- **Answer Questions:** Start answering questions asked within the forums. Do NOT post adverts for your web site or products. Use this time to establish your credentials. If you answer questions well and contribute to the forums, your web site tag will be noticed.
- **Set up a PPC campaign** – you can start with the smaller search engines first. Take your very small advert and your keywords and use them in your campaign. Most search engines will help you with your choice of keywords. Remember to set a budget and test, test and test again until you get quality and converting traffic.
- **Test, Update and Modify.** Review, change and add to your PPC keywords. Submit more articles and adverts. Start tactfully promoting your products in the forums.

Well that's what to do to be a success. Good Luck.

Profitable New Quilting Business

Expanding

Expansion means growth, involving people working for you, more jobs to sell, and greater profits. Don't let it frighten you, for you have gained experience by starting gradually. After all - your aim in starting a business of your own was to make money, wasn't it? And expanding means more helpers so you don't have to work your self to death!

Staff

So, just as soon as you possibly can, recruit and hire other people to do the work for you. The first people you hire should be people to handle the basic work that you do..

You can obtain good staff by word of mouth, advertising in your local Job Centre, supermarket etc. Look in your local university and local school and ask amongst friends.

You will find a lot of people who want to work part time here which you will need at the start of your business.

Profitable New Quilting Business

You can start these people at minimum wage or a bit above, and train them to complete every job assignment in two hours or less. You might consider hiring people on a contract basis so that if they don't work you don't pay. You don't get loyalty here though.

You should also outfit them in a kind of uniform with your company name on the back of their blouses or shirts. A good idea would be to have magnetic signs made for your company and services. Place these signs on the sides of the cars your people use for transportation to each job, and later on, the sides of your company van or pick-up trucks.

Advertising

A good supply of business cards wouldn't be a bad idea for them either, in order to advertise your services to others they come in contact with. The only other form of advertising you should go with would be a display ad in the yellow pages of your telephone directory.

Customer Contracts

When you're dealing with customers, sometimes things can go wrong. It might be your fault, it might be their fault or it might be no-one's fault -- but if you didn't make a contract, then you'll all suffer.

Why Do I Need Contracts?

A contract gives you a sound legal base for your business, and some guarantee that you're going to get paid for your work without you having to ask the customer for payment in advance. In the event of a dispute, the contract lays down what the agreement was so that you can point to it and say what was agreed. If you ever end up having to go to court (let's hope you won't), the contract is what the judge's decision will be based on.

Profitable New Quilting Business

Without a contract, you leave yourself vulnerable and open to exploitation. Someone could claim that the terms they agreed with you were different to what you say they were or that they never signed up for anything at all and so they won't pay.

It's especially common to see big businesses mistreat small ones, thinking that they won't have the knowledge or the money to do anything about it. Essentially, contracts take away your customers' ability to hold non-payment over your head, and give you the ability to hold it over theirs instead.

Written and Verbal Contracts

It is important to point out the distinction in the law between a verbal (spoken) contract and a proper, written one. A verbal contract is binding in theory, but in practice can be very hard to prove. A written contract, on the other hand, is rock-solid proof of what you're saying.

You might think that you're never going to get into a dispute with your customers, but it's all too common to find yourself in a little disagreement. They will often want to get you to do some 'small' amount of extra work to finish the job or make it better; not realizing that doing so would completely obliterate your profit margin.

For this reason, you should be very wary of doing anything with nothing but a verbal contract. On the other hand, if you were incautious or too trusting and only got a verbal contract, it could still go some way towards helping you, especially if there were witnesses.

Won't It Be Expensive?

Written contracts don't necessarily need to be formal contracts, which are drawn up by a lawyer with 'contract' written at the top and signed by both parties.

These kinds of contracts are the most effective, but can be expensive to have produced, not to mention intimidating to customers.

Profitable New Quilting Business

The most common kind of written contract, oddly enough, is a simple letter. If you send a customer a letter laying out your agreement before you start work, and they write back to agree to it, that is enough to qualify as a written contract, with most of the protections it affords. It is best to get confirmation from your customer that they have received this contract.

If you are doing high-value work for some clients, though, it could be worth the time and trouble of having your lawyer write a formal contract, or at least of doing it yourself and getting a lawyer to look it over.

Formal contracts will give you more protection if the worst happens, and there's nothing to stop you from making it a one-off expense only by re-using the same contract for multiple customers. PLEASE: TAKE PROFESSIOANAL ADVICE.

Contracts for Small Purchases.

Obviously it would be silly to expect everyone who buys some £10 product or service from you to sign a contract, or write back indicating their agreement to your terms. In this situation, you should have a statement of the 'terms and conditions' that your customer is agreeing to by buying from you, and they should have to tick some kind of box indicating their agreement before you send anything.

Profitable New Quilting Business

The Top 5 First-Year Mistakes

Even once you've got past the starting-up stage, there are still plenty mistakes to be made, and most of them are going to be made in your make-or-break year -- the first one. Here are the top five things to avoid.

Waiting for Customers to Come to You

Too many people wait for their customers to phone, or come to the door, or whatever. They get one or two customers through luck, but nothing like enough to even begin paying their costs. These people sit around, looking at their competitors doing lots of business, and wonder what they're doing wrong.

You can't be like this. You have to go out there and actively try to find customers. Talk to people, call them, meet with them -- whatever you do, don't just sit there!

Spending Too Much on Advertising

So everyone tells you that the only way to get ahead in business is to advertise. Well, that's true, but you need to make sure that you stick to inexpensive advertising methods when you're starting out. Spending hundreds of dollars for an ad in the local newspaper might turn out to get you very few new customers, and you will have spent your entire advertising budget on it.

Make your money go further with leaflets, direct mail or email -- these are easily targetable campaign methods with high response rates and low costs. Remember that it is always better to spend money on an offer than on an ad, and always better to spend money on an ad than on a delivery method.

Being Too Nice

When you're running your own business, it can be tempting to be everyone's friend, giving discounts at the drop of a hat and making sure that you don't hassle or inconvenience anyone.

Profitable New Quilting Business

That's all well and good, until you find that your Good Samaritan act has just halved your profit margin without lowering the cost to the customer by very much at all.

Sometimes, you need to realize that you've got to be harsh to make a profit. Give people discounts to encourage them to buy or to come back, not because you like them or feel sorry for them. Don't be afraid to be ruthless in your pursuit of business success. Nice guys don't finish last, but they are running in a different race -- one with much less prize money. If that doesn't bother you, of course, then feel free to go for it.

Not Using the Phone

You'd be surprised just how common phone fears are -- if you're scared of the phone, you're not alone by any means. Many people are terrified of making phone calls, and avoid them wherever possible. I have seen more than one business owner reduced to tears on the phone and trying desperately to hide it from the customer.

Profitable New Quilting Business

You need to try your best to overcome your fears, as talking to customers on the phone is almost as good as meeting them for real. Letters and emails are useless by comparison. The best way to overcome phone fears varies from person to person, but it can often be as simple as making the phone fun, by calling friends and relatives often for a while and getting used to it. Alternatively, try working in telemarketing for a while -- if that doesn't make normal phone use look like a walk in the park by comparison, then nothing will.

Hiring Professionals for Everything

It can be tempting to think that, since you're starting out, you should just find a company or person to do every little thing you need. People seem to especially overspend on design services.

Profitable New Quilting Business

You might think it'd be great to have fancy graphics all over your website, but would it really increase sales? If I saw it, it would put me right off. Likewise, a slick brochure often fails to say anything more than 'I'm going to charge you a premium to pay for my expensive brochures'. Don't hire someone unless you can demonstrate that the service they're going to provide will increase your profits by more than the amount you're spending -- if you're not sure, try it yourself first, and you can always upgrade it later.

Problems You May Have

As in any business you will get problems, sometimes just knowing what you may face is a great help.

- Some customers use office email to correspond with you. Make sure that you are discrete with the headings used on the emails to them.
- Some customers are never satisfied. Just make any reasonable changes that are requested. Be polite and patient.
- Some customers may have problems explaining what they want – this is where your product sheet comes in handy. Make sure that you write down everything that they request and get this agreed to.
- Some customers are very slow in replying – ensure that you give them a time limit to reply and then send two further reminders – telling them when the last one is.

Profitable New Quilting Business

Time for a Holiday: But How?

When you've been working long and hard at your business for a while, you might feel like you've earned yourself a little break. There are business owners out there who haven't taken a real holiday since they started their business -- including some who started their business as long as five years ago!

After all, how can you ever just desert your business and your customers and go bronze yourself on the beach? How can you avoid being on call 24/7 throughout your holiday? Well, everyone deserves some time to themselves at least once a year, if they want to keep being productive and avoid stress. Here's what to do.

Tell People When You Are Going Away.

You can't just disappear when you're running a business -- you need to let people know long in advance that you're not going to be available, and make sure that they have everything they need to manage without you while you're away. It's best to schedule your holiday not to interfere too much with the business.

However much you might want to have your holiday in the summer, it's important to remember that every business has its quiet months, and you should schedule your holiday in the period where they seem to be.

Change Your Voicemail Message.

A quick and simple way to let people know that you've gone away is to change your voicemail message.

This allows you to still hear what people have to say when you get back, and stops them from wondering why you never seem to answer your phone.

A good format for the message is as follows: 'Hi, this is [your name] at [company name]. I'm sorry I'm not in the office right now, but I will be back on [give a date]. If you leave a message, I will be sure to get back to you'.

If you work from home don't give a coming back date unless you want to invite the local thief into your home!

Set Up an Email Auto responder.

Similar to a voicemail message, but less commonly used, is the email auto responder. Again, you don't want people to wonder why their emails are going unanswered, so your best bet is to set up your email program to automatically reply to any email you get with a message saying that you've gone away.

Example: 'Hello, and thank you for your email. This is an auto responder, as I'm away on holiday until [date]. I have received your email, however, and will respond to it upon my return. I apologies for any inconvenience to you, and I am willing to make an offer of 10% off your next order to make it up to you.' The special offer for people who get the auto responder is a nice touch -- it makes them feel lucky that they emailed you while you were away, instead of frustrated.

Profitable New Quilting Business

Don't Stay Away Too Long.

Of course, when you go on holiday, you're relying on people being willing to wait for you. That means you can't really take the kids to Disney World for two weeks, or spend a month staying with a friend abroad -- it's just too long to be away from your business for. You should regard a weekend away as ideal (it avoids the whole problem for the most part), and a week as the maximum you can allow yourself. Don't let people make you feel bad about only taking one-week holidays: after all, you could always have more than one each year.

Get Someone to Look after the Business.

If you really want to get away for longer, or it's essential that your customers don't have any break in service, then you could consider getting someone to look after your business. This could be an existing member of staff that you make your 'deputy', to be in charge while you're away, or it could be someone who's related to you and has some experience running a business.

Profitable New Quilting Business

In Conclusion

One of the most important aspects of this business is asking for, and allowing your customers to refer other prospects to you. All of this happens, of course, as a result of your giving fast, dependable service. You might even set up a promotional notice on the back of your business card (to be left as each job is completed) offering five dollars off their next bill when they refer you to a new prospect.

This is definitely a high profit business, requiring only an investment of time and organisation on your part to get started. With a low investment, little or no over head requirement, and no experience needed, this is an ideal business opportunity with a growth curve that accelerates at an unprecedented rate. Think about it. If it appeals to you, set up your own plan of operations and go for it! The profit potential for an owner of this type of business is outstanding! Good Luck.

Quilting Terminology

Some of the terminology for quilting that you will find useful is given below:

Accent quilting can add pattern that works with, but follows, different lines to those of any patchwork.

Achromatic colour schemes - using black white and grey only

Album quilts – these use a mix of blocks pertinent to the maker, the recipient or an event, and are usually gifts for specific events or circumstances

Amish Quilts – these are very simplistic and orderly and always functional

Analogous colour schemes – neighbouring colours on a colour wheel

Profitable New Quilting Business

Anchor fabric – this is used when piecing to hold the fabric pieces together when machine piecing

Appliqué – not specific to quilting, but often used on quilts – this is the use of smaller pieces of fabric, often making a figure or character, stitched to the face fabric of the quilt. Sun Bonnett Sue's are examples of these. Various stitches can be used – visible or invisible

Backing fabric – as you would expect, this is this is the base fabric

Bargello quilting – use of fabric strips to give the look of a wave

Basting is a way of holding the three sandwich layers together on a temporary basis. You can tack, pin or use sticky spray

Batting is the middle or wadding layer of your quilt sandwich

Bearding is when the batting fibbers come away and find their way through to the face or base fabric – it happens more with polyester wadding.

Beeswax coating on thread makes it stronger and prevents it from knotting.

Betweens are quilting needles, and they are very short. Sizes 9, 10 or 12 are generally used – the 12 being longer than the nine.

Binding is used to create the quilt edges. It is essential to cut binding on the bias to avoid pulling out of shape.

Blanket stitch – originally used to edge blankets and prevent fraying, it is also used as a decorative stitch for securing pieces of appliqué

Block – a section of patchwork, usually, but not always, square

Border – fabric strips used between blocks and or on the top bottom and sides.

Profitable New Quilting Business

Cats ears – a block style also known as prairie points

Chain sewing- a continual thread to sew pieces together without finishing off and re-starting

Chain stitch – is an embroidery stitch that resembles a chain.

Charm quilts have only one shape which is used repeatedly, but never using the same fabric more than once

Cheaters Cloth – fabric which looks like it is made of patchwork, but which is actually printed

Cool colours – blues or greens

Crazy quilt – quilt using irregular fabric pieces stitched to foundation fabric and then decorated.

Cross hatch – parallel lines marked on the quilt to help hand stitching.

Cross hatching uses straight lines on a grid – diamonds or square or rectangles can be used.

Dimensional appliqué – this stands in relief from the quilt cover, either stuffed or not.

Profitable New Quilting Business

Echo quilting – lines of quilting that repeat around the edge of a piece or design

Fat Quarter is a yard and a half of fabric cut in half to enable a square piece 18" x 22"

Foundation blocks are blocks that are made up of any number of small pieces of fabric. The finished block is then joined to other finished blocks to create the patchwork face. Try and keep the fabric, if possible, to have the straight grain on the edge of the block.

Frames can be small circular hoops for hand sewing or large rectangular frames for holding bigger quilts.

Friendship quilt – made to be given to friends or family and often having messages or using swap fabric

Grain – the line of fibber running perpendicular to the side selvedge

Hawaiian appliqué – A technique for applying very detailed design pieces onto quilt fabric.

Hoops – large frames to hold the quilt for hand or machine stitching

Lap quilting – quilting squares as complete pieces, and then joining the pieces when they are all made

Lattice strips – strips bordering the blocks

Loft – the spare between face and the backing fabrics – high lofts mean warmer, thicker quilts

Meandering or stippling style – this is a style of filling in areas of quilt with stitch, but none of the stitching should touch. So you can't cross over a line you have already stitched

Marking – marking the quilt by tracing or freehand to indicate where to stitch the quilt. Tailors chalk or wax is often used – soap also works.

Medallion quilt – a quilt with a central design from which the rest of the design follows outwards

Millennium quilts - or Y2K quilts – to commemorate the year 2000

Mitres – a method of measuring diagonals and angles

Monochromatic – all one colour

Motif stitching gives a pattern which can be done on plain or patch work quilting. Motifs allow the quilter to incorporate names, hearts, animals, flowers, in fact any object, or, an abstract pattern.

Profitable New Quilting Business

Muslin – a very thin plain fabric, often used as a foundation fabric for piecing blocks

No knots – No knots are to be seen when quilting. The trick is to pull the knot through to the batting layer so that it can be hidden. When you finish you will also need to lose your knot in the centre batting. As with a starter knot, wrap the cotton a couple of times round the needle, check your last stitch hole, and pop the needle back in, and pull it through so that the knot stops in the batting, then cut the thread close to the fabric.

Off hand – usually the left hand which guides the needle from underneath the quilt

Outline stitching is, as you would expect, intended to provide an outline, and achieved by stitching about ¼ away from the seam. By doing this, the quilt is strengthened, as you get, in effect, a double line of stitching, and the other advantage is that the stitching is inside the cut edge and no seal allowance is needed.

Paper piecing – using paper to attach pieces in a block. The paper is usually numbered or lettered and the pieces are matched, stitched to the paper and the adjoining pieces.

Piecing – stitching pieces of fabric together – or called patchwork

Quilting Thread is single strand of very strong cotton and glazed to help it pass through the batting.

Rocking – this is the popular method – if you rock the needle back and forth you should be able to get about 4 or 5 stitches on at one go.

Sampler – showing a number of different quilting techniques

Sashing – fabric strips that separate blocks

Satin Stitch – side by side stitching

Selvedge – the edges of the fabric where the weave was finished.

Seminole quilting – creating large pieces of fabric with pieces so that the joined fabric can then be cut and used with shapes repeated.

Sewing in the ditch refers to stitching very close to a seam where the stitches are barely visible.

Sharps – fine needles for joining pieces and stitching on appliqué

Stencil – using a pre made shape for transferring designs and motifs

Template – a shape for cutting pieces – made of plastic, paper, sandpaper.

Warm colours – orange, red, yellows and tans

Index

advertising, 25, 30, 65

appliqué, 43, 45, 57, 58, 59, 60, 108, 109, 111, 115

Banking, 23, 71

batting, 47, 54, 55, 56, 107, 113, 114

brand, 26, 33, 65, 66, 67

Branding, 33, 66

business cards, 26, 69, 89

Business Name, 21

business plan, 14

Business Plan, 19, 23

capital, 8, 30

Celebration Quilts, 34

contract, 76, 77, 78, 89, 90, 91, 92, 93, 94

Customer Administration, 72

Distribution, 32

distributor, 25, 26, 32, 65

Estimating, 76

information pack, 13, 69, 78

Insurance, 22

Internet, 79

Invoices, 66

lease, 24, 25

Legal Base, 19

Licenses, 22

licensing, 13

loans, 27

marketing, 16, 17, 18, 20, 23, 24, 25, 26, 29, 30, 67, 68, 83, 84, 85

Marketing Material, 67

Order Forms, 66, 67

Packaging, 65, 66, 67

Profitable New Quilting Business

Patents and Trademarks, 22
patterns, 47, 48, 50, 61
Permits, 22
Planning, 17
price points, 30
Pricing, 65
Quilting stencils, 61, 62
Quilting templates, 63
Staff, 20, 26, 71, 88

Staff costs, 26
Stock, 26, 33
stock levels, 65
Strategy, 16, 83, 84, 85
Taxes, 22
Uniforms, 26
upgrades, 30
wadding, 47, 107
web site, 20, 21, 66, 67, 79, 80, 81, 82
Your Market, 19

Profitable New Quilting Business